Life in the UK Test Prep | 2023 Edition:

The Most Complete Guide to Become a British citizen and pass the exam on the first try with Practice Questions and Secrets from an Expert in the Field

Rob Blacksmith

Table of Contents

Introduction

Most persons now need to pass "The Life in the UK Test" to live permanently in the United Kingdom (UK) or receive British citizenship. About 160,000 people take the test each year.

Since the new course study materials were introduced in March 2013, there is no information available on pass rates. The former test's average pass rates had increased year on year, reaching a peak of 86 percent. If the new test is harder than anticipated, pass rates could drop down to a level of 75%. (a 1 in 4 failure rate). Thai nationals have historically fared poorly on the exam, with an average pass rate of only about 50%.

Thais who read this book should be able to ace the Life in the UK exam. There is no need for another study guide because this one has an exact replication of the "official study materials" on which the test is based.

The booklet has practice questions, revision materials, and information on what to anticipate from the test to help you get ready.

In the UK, the topic of migration is current. The visa categories and procedures that lead to settlement in the UK are constantly being modified by succeeding governments. While the current visa rules are summarized in this book, readers are urged to consult their advisor or the UK Border and Immigration website for the most up-to-date information.

Examples of the kinds of questions you might encounter if you ever need to attend an interview for a British passport are also provided in this tutorial.

Choosing to become a citizen of the UK is an exciting choice that thousands of individuals annually make. The decision to obtain British citizenship or permanent residency, however, merely marks the beginning of what may be a protracted and difficult process. The application procedure is difficult, expensive, and time-consuming.

According to Home Office data, almost three out of ten test takers failed in 2014. This is an expensive and unnecessary mistake, costing £50 for each test taken. According to customer feedback, 93% of people succeed on their first try.

The Life in the UK Test is taken by tens of thousands of people each year, although not all of them succeed. But if you prepare properly, you can be one of the people who succeeds on the first try.

Chapter 1:
History Of The UK

The first settlers in Britain during the so-called Stone Age were hunter-gatherers. Britain and the continent were connected by a land bridge for the majority of the Stone Age. Following the herds of horses and animals they hunted, people came and went. It took the Channel about 10,000 years to completely divide Britain from the continent.

About 6,000 years ago, the country of Britain received its first farmers. These earliest farmers most likely came from Southeast Europe. On the land, these people erected residences, cemeteries, and memorials. Stonehenge, one of these structures, is still standing today in Wiltshire, an English county. Probably used as a unique location for seasonal ceremonies, Stonehenge. There are a few additional Stone Age sites as well. The best-preserved prehistoric settlement in northern Europe is located on the Scottish island of Orkney, and it is from this location that archaeologists have learned more about how people lived towards the end of the Stone Age.

People initially figured out how to manufacture bronze some 4,000 years ago. This time frame is known as the Bronze Age. Roundhouses were used as homes, and round barrows served as graveyards. The bronze period metalworkers produced a wide range of exquisite tools, jewelry, and weapons made of bronze and gold. After the Bronze Age, when humanity first discovered how to forge iron into tools and weapons, came the Iron Age. People continued to occupy larger towns, dwell in roundhouses, and occasionally defend fortifications on hillsides. In the English county of Dorset, there is a hill fort at Maiden Castle that is still well visible. The majority of people worked as farmers, artisans, or soldiers. They spoke a language that was a member of the Celtic language family. During the Iron Age, similar languages were used throughout Europe; some regions of Wales, Scotland, and Ireland still speak kindred tongues today. The Iron Age population possessed a highly developed culture and economy.

What is the UK?

The UK (United Kingdom) is a country located in Europe, consisting of four countries: England, Scotland, Wales, and Northern Ireland. It is a constitutional monarchy, meaning it has a monarch (currently Queen Elizabeth II) as the head of state, but its political system is democratic. The UK has a rich history and culture, and is known for its contributions to science, literature, music, and many other fields. Its capital city is London, and the official language is English. The UK is also a member of international organizations such as the United Nations, NATO, and the European Union (although it left the EU in 2020).

Geography

In the northwest of continental Europe, there is a sovereign state called the United Kingdom (UK or U.K.). It used to be physically connected to the continent of Europe via land, but the English Channel now stands between them. A tunnel spans the English Channel from Folkstone in southeast England to Coquelles in Pas-de-Calais in northern France.

Great Britain is the collective name for England, Wales, and Scotland. The "United Kingdom of Great Britain and Northern Ireland" is made up of the following countries: England, Wales, Scotland, and Northern Ireland. The capital of each nation is located in one of Belfast, Edinburgh, Cardiff, or London. Quite a few counties make up the United Kingdom. Counties not only divide people geographically but also politically, socially, and occasionally culturally.

Three tiny islands are referred to as "Crown Dependencies" even though they are not technically a part of the United Kingdom. These are the English Channel's Isle of Man and the Channel Islands, which also include Jersey and Guernsey (which is in the Irish Sea). They may be controlled individually and are essentially autonomous. British Overseas Territories are 14 more countries that are governed by the UK but are not Crown Dependencies.

London, the capital and largest city of the United Kingdom, is a prominent worldwide financial hub with a metro population of around 10 million. Birmingham (England), Liverpool (England), Leeds (England), Manchester (England), Glasgow (Scotland), Cardiff (Wales), and Belfast are some of the most important UK cities (Northern Ireland).

The Queen and her duties and roles

Her Majesty Queen Elizabeth II is the reigning monarch at the moment. In 1952, when she was proclaimed as monarch, she set a new record for the longest-reigning head of state in history. She had already devoted her young life to serving her country during World War II. The Queen performs significant ceremonial and formal duties for the UK government as well as significant roles in the devolved legislatures of Wales, Scotland, and Northern Ireland as well as the UK parliament in London. She must, however, uphold her political neutrality in her capacity as head of state today. The Church of England and the military forces are both under the control of the Queen. She is also in charge of New Zealand, Australia, and Canada.

The head of state and designated spokesman for the UK on issues relating to national identity and cultural concerns is Queen Elizabeth. One of the constitutional monarchies is the British monarchy. In other words, although if the Sovereign is the Head of State, the power to make and carry out laws rests with a Parliament chosen by the general populace. As a result, Parliament is in charge of overseeing the country's everyday activities (not the Queen). The Sovereign continues to play a vital role in national life even after giving up political or governmental office.

Political parties

In the unitary parliamentary democracy of the UK, voting is encouraged but not mandated. There are many political parties, but the two biggest are the Labor Party and the Conservative and Unionist Party (also known as the Tory Party or the Tories).

Government

The United Kingdom is governed by a parliament that convenes in central London's Westminster. With authority delegated from the UK Parliament, which has the power to introduce laws to amend or even end devolution, Wales, Scotland, and Northern Ireland each have their own devolved governments. Parliament is made up of the House of Commons and the House of Lords. These Houses of Parliament are responsible for passing legislation, setting tax rates, and scrutinizing the executive branch.

Local government would be regarded as a lesser level of government because it operates at the county and even town levels.

Time zone

The UK observes Greenwich Mean Time (GMT), which is identical to UTC, during the winter (Universally Coordinated Time). The UK observes daylight savings time in the summer (known as British Summer Time or BST). On the final Sunday in March, at 2 a.m., the clocks move forward one hour officially. Even if you don't agree with the concept of daylight savings time, you cannot object to this because it is a legislative obligation. So, for instance, on Sunday, March 29, 2020, at 2:00 a.m., the clocks were set ahead one hour. You would have "lost" an hour of sleep that night as a result. On the last Sunday in October, the clocks switch back to GMT for the winter. For instance, in 2020, the time change occurred on Sunday, October 25, at 2:00 a.m. You would have "gained" an hour of sleep that night as a result.

Chapter 2:
Values And Principles Of The UK

Values are the standards that a group of people or an individual uphold. They are a civilization's defining traits as well as who and what they believe individuals should be. All UK residents uphold a set of fundamental principles, such as democracy, the parliamentary system, the defense of human rights, freedom of speech and religion, gender equality, and tolerance for those who have differing opinions from their own.

The state is an organization made up of the people that live in each nation.

The state is made up of a confederation of separate entities that are linked by a treaty.

Within a state, democracy is the only system of government and set of laws.

The people, who are also the source of political power, have the authority to make laws and choose a government to implement them.

According to the human rights law, which is safeguarded by a treaty or international law, every person has rights and freedoms.

The rule of law is upheld by the courts as a population management strategy.

Along with equality, liberty, freedom, and justice, the idea of democracy as the cornerstone of governance is one of the tenets of British civilization. In a democracy, the people are in power and there is a form of representative government. The Magna Carta, which stated that the King may only rule with the permission of his or her subjects, was passed in 1215, establishing the foundation for the British democratic system more than a thousand years ago. The Glorious Revolution of 1688, which was a turning point in the growth of contemporary democracy, enhanced democracy in England.

Democracy is viewed as a fair and open form of government in the UK. The House of Commons elections are open to everyone, regardless of gender, nationality, or religion.

Understanding our beliefs and the driving forces behind our conduct may help us better comprehend who we are as people. We may decide what is best for a society, talk about the concepts and tenets that underpin them, and help clarify any potential repercussions that a certain value may have.

In British politics, the Chamber of Commons is referred to as "the lowest house of the legislature." It can only serve as a representative of the community if it is chosen by all voters. The finest candidates in each constituency are picked by the voters to represent them in Westminster in a general election that takes place every five years. Even though it lacks legislative authority, the Chamber of Lords, an elected upper house in the United Kingdom, primarily serves as a check on what the "Lower House" approves. The prime minister and the remainder of the cabinet, including any junior officials, are chosen by the lower house of parliament.

The Magna Carta, due process, and other constitutional principles are deeply ingrained in British political culture even though the British constitution is not codified. The United Kingdom has accepted the European Convention on Human Rights, an international accord that protects fundamental freedoms and human rights in Europe.

Without a warrant, no one may be detained or brought into custody unless there are extreme circumstances that make it impossible to wait for the individual to arrive.

Within 24 hours, the police must alert the court bailiff and the home secretary of this. Article 9 of the European Convention on Human Rights, which ensures a fair trial, is consistent with this. Within 24 hours, the court bailiff must also affirm this to the home secretary, who must then inform the police that they need not take any further action because they are confident the arrest was lawful. Even while not all arrests necessitate warrants, all warrants require advance notice of this procedure.

Each and every detainee has the right to contact or chat with a relative or counsel. The individual must be informed of their right to contact someone and given the chance to do so by the police.

A person must be told of the charge in a language they can comprehend when they are detained and charged with a crime. Due to the Police and Criminal Evidence (PACE) Act in Northern Ireland, police in England, Wales, and Scotland are not allowed to give legal advice or warnings to suspects as of August 1, 2005. If the suspect is unable to understand English, the document needs to be translated for them.

Fantastic place to call home, with an illustrious past and a thriving, contemporary civilization. The evolution of the global political, scientific, industrial, and cultural systems has been largely influenced by our people. We take pride in our tradition of embracing new immigrants who will broaden the diversity and vitality of our country.

A significant investment is needed to submit applications for citizenship or permanent residency in the UK. You agree to support UK laws, values, and customs by accepting the obligations of permanent residency. An benefit for the UK is having good citizens. Anyone who wishes to make a difference in our society is welcome here.

The human rights law, which is safeguarded by a treaty or international law, grants each and every person certain rights and liberties.

As a tool of managing the public, the courts uphold the rule of law.

Along with equality, liberty, freedom, and justice, one of the cornerstones of British civilization is the idea of democracy as the basis for government. Democracies are a form of representational government where the populace is in charge. With the passing of the Magna Carta in 1215, which ruled that the King may only rule with the permission of his or her subjects, the British democratic system was created more than a thousand years ago. During the Glorious Revolution of 1688, which was a watershed moment in the evolution of contemporary democracy, democracy was enhanced in England.

Democracy is viewed as an honest and fair system of government in the UK. No matter a person's gender, nationality, or religion, they can cast a vote in the House of Commons elections.

By comprehending our ideas and the driving forces behind our conduct, we would be better equipped to comprehend who we are as people. We may choose what is best for a society, debate the theories and precepts that underpin them, and assist in illuminating any potential effects that a certain value may have.

British politics refers to the House of Commons as "the lowest house of the legislature." Only if every eligible voter chooses it will it truly represent the community. Every five years, the voters of each constituency elect the top candidates to represent them in Westminster in a general election. Despite not having legislative authority, the UK's elected upper house, the Chamber of Lords, primarily serves as a check on what the "Lower House" approves. The lower house of parliament chooses the rest of the government, including any junior officials, as well as the prime minister.

Many constitutional ideas, including the rule of law, due process, and the Magna Carta, are ingrained in British political culture despite the fact that the British constitution is not codified. The United Kingdom has accepted the European Convention on Human Rights, a treaty that protects fundamental freedoms and human rights in Europe.

Except in extreme cases where it would be impossible to wait for the person's arrival, no one may be detained or brought into custody without a warrant.

This must be reported by the police to the Home Secretary and court bailiff within 24 hours. This is in line with the guarantee of a fair trial under Article 9 of the European Convention on Human Rights. Within 24 hours, the court bailiff must also affirm this to the home secretary, who must then inform the police that they can rest easy knowing that the arrest was lawful and that no further action is necessary. Even while not all arrests require warrants, all warrants for arrest, when necessary, require advance notice of this procedure.

Every single inmate has the right to contact or chat with a family member or counsel. The subject must be informed by the police of their right to contact someone and given the chance to do so.

When someone is arrested and accused of a crime, they must be given the charge's details in a language they can understand. Since August 1, 2005, the Police and Criminal Evidence (PACE) Act in Northern Ireland has prohibited police in England, Wales, and Scotland from providing suspects with legal counsel or warnings. If the suspect is unable to read English, a translation of the document is required.

Fantastic place to call home, with a rich past and a modern society that is thriving. The world's political, scientific, industrial, and cultural systems have all been shaped by the contributions of our people. We take pride in the history of opening our doors to new immigrants who will broaden the diversity and vitality of our country.

Making the effort to apply for citizenship in the UK or as a permanent resident is time-consuming. You hereby agree to support the laws, beliefs, and traditions of the UK and to assume the obligations of permanent residency. The UK benefits from having good citizens. Anyone who want to make a contribution to our society is welcome.

The values and principles of the UK

All UK citizens ought to respect and support the fundamental principles and beliefs that guide British society. These values represent the duties, privileges, and rights that come with being a citizen or long-term resident of the UK. They are founded on history and traditions and backed by laws, social norms, and expectations. In British society, extremism and bigotry have no place.

Chapter 3:
Modern UK Society And Culture

The UK today

Today's United Kingdom is more diverse in terms of race and religion than it was a century ago. Due to post-war immigration, about 10% of people have a parent or grandparent who was born outside of the UK. The UK is still a multiracial society with an extensive and varied cultural heritage. The major UK regions as well as a number of significant localities are covered in this section. Additionally, some of the more well-known occasions and several UK customs and traditions will be covered.

The nations of the UK

The UK (United Kingdom) is composed of four countries: England, Scotland, Wales, and Northern Ireland. Each country has its own distinct culture, history, and traditions, and together they form a rich and diverse nation.

England is the largest and most populous country in the UK, and its capital city is London. Scotland is the northernmost country, with Edinburgh as its capital. Wales is located to the west of England, and its capital is Cardiff. Northern Ireland is located on the island of Ireland, and its capital is Belfast.

Each country has its own government and parliament, except for England, which is governed directly by the UK parliament in Westminster. However, there are ongoing debates and discussions about devolving more powers to each of the individual countries.

Cities of the UK

The United Kingdom (UK) is home to numerous cities, each with its own distinct character and history. Some of the major cities in the UK include:

London - the capital of the UK and one of the most vibrant and diverse cities in the world. It is a global hub for business, finance, culture, and education.

Manchester - a vibrant city in the north of England, known for its music scene, football clubs, and thriving arts and culture.

Liverpool - a historic city on the west coast of England, famous for being the birthplace of the Beatles and for its iconic waterfront.

Birmingham - the second-largest city in the UK, located in the heart of England. It is known for its industrial heritage and is home to a number of museums and galleries.

Edinburgh - the capital of Scotland, known for its stunning architecture, vibrant cultural scene, and famous festivals.

Glasgow - Scotland's largest city, known for its industrial heritage, music scene, and world-class museums.

Cardiff - the capital of Wales, a vibrant city known for its historic castle, modern waterfront, and thriving arts and culture.

Belfast - the capital of Northern Ireland, a vibrant city with a rich history and a burgeoning arts and culture scene.

Other notable cities in the UK include Bristol, Leeds, Newcastle, Sheffield, Nottingham, and Southampton, among others.

Languages and dialects

The various regions of the United Kingdom speak a wide variety of languages. There are numerous accents and dialects used in English. Welsh is a widely used language in Wales that is entirely distinct from English and is taught in schools and institutions. Irish Gaelic is spoken by some Northern Irish people, and Gaelic is also spoken by some Highland and Island Scots (again, a separate language).

Population

The population of the UK has changed over time, as seen in the table below.

In recent years, the population has been growing more quickly. Population increase is influenced by immigration to the UK and longer life expectancies.

The population distribution within the UK's four regions is incredibly uneven. More than 84 percent of the population lives in England, with Wales making up around 5 percent, Scotland a little more than 8 percent, and Northern Ireland less than 3 percent.

An ageing population

People are living longer than ever in the UK. Higher living standards and better healthcare are to blame for this. Today, a record number of people are over the age of 85. This has an effect on healthcare and pension expenditures.

Ethnic diversity

The ethnic makeup of the UK population is diverse and rapidly changing, especially in big centres like London. It's not always simple to determine everyone's ethnic background.

People from many different ethnic groups can be found in the UK. White people, who include those with European, Australian, Canadian, New Zealander, and American ancestry, are the most frequently selected ethnic group in surveys. Persons of Asian, Black, and Mixed racial background are among other noteworthy groups.

An equal society

It is illegal in the UK to treat men and women differently because of their gender or marital status. They have the right to employment, property ownership, marriage, and divorce. If the parents are married, they each have a parenting role to play.

Women currently make up about half of the workforce in Britain. Girls typically graduate from high school with more certificates than boys do. University students are typically more female than male.

Women now have a lot more employment options than they did in the past. Women work in every division of the organization, and in fields where men have traditionally dominated the workforce, more women than ever hold prominent managerial positions. Compared to the past, men work in a larger variety of professions today.

Women are no longer expected to stay at home and refrain from working. Many women carry on working after having children. Many families today have two working parents who split the duties of childcare and housework.

Religion

The United Kingdom has long been a Christian nation. 59 percent of respondents to the 2011 Census declared themselves to be Christians. Muslims made up the bulk of the population (4.8%), followed by Hindus (1.5%), Sikhs (0.8%), Jews, and Buddhists (both less than 0.5 percent). All around the UK, there are places of worship for various religious traditions. This comprises Buddhist temples, Hindu temples, Sikh gurdwaras, and Jewish synagogues. Nevertheless, it is legal for anyone to choose their faith or not. 25% of respondents to the 2011 census indicated that they did not practice any religion.

The main Christian festivals

In the UK, a number of significant Christian holidays are observed. Some of the most significant ones are listed below:

Christmas is one of the most significant holidays in the Christian calendar since it marks the birth of Jesus Christ. Every year on December 25, it is observed.

Easter is the second-most significant Christian holiday after Christmas and commemorates the death and resurrection of Jesus Christ. The first Sunday following the first full moon following the vernal equinox is when Easter is observed (usually between March 22 and April 25).

Before Easter, a 40-day period known as Lent is a time for fasting, prayer, and repentance. On Ash Wednesday, Lent begins, and it lasts until Holy Saturday.

Pentecost - This holiday commemorates the moment, 50 days after Easter, when the Holy Spirit descended upon the apostles. It is often referred to as Whit Sunday or Whitsun.

The day known as All Saints' Day is set aside to honor all the martyrs and saints of the Christian faith. The first of November is the holiday.

The day known as All Souls' Day is devoted to honoring the pious gone. On November 2nd, it is observed.

Good Friday is commemorated as a day of grief and reflection as it commemorates the day that Jesus Christ was crucified. On the Friday before Easter, it is observed.

There are numerous other festivals and holy days that Christians observe throughout the year in addition to these popular ones in the UK.

Other religious festivals

Diwali is a five-day festival that typically occurs in October or November. The Festival of Lights is the name given to it. It is observed by Hindus and Sikhs alike. It honors knowledge and the triumph of right over wrong. There are various origin tales for the festival. Leicester hosts a well-known Diwali celebration.

Hanukkah, which lasts for eight days, is observed in November or December. It brings to mind the Jewish fight for religious tolerance. A candle is lighted on a menorah, an eight-candle stand, on each day of the holiday to commemorate the legend of how oil that was meant to last for one day instead lasted for eight.

Muslims celebrate Eid al-Fitr to honor the completion of Ramadan, during which they fasted for one month. They express gratitude to Allah for granting them the stamina to finish the fast. Each year, a new day is chosen for the event. Muslims partake in rituals and feasts that are unique to them.

Eid ul Adha celebrates the prophet Ibrahim's readiness to offer his son as a sacrifice when God required it. It tries to reaffirm Muslims' own devotion to God. At this event, many Muslims sacrifice an animal to eat. This must be carried out in a slaughterhouse in Britain.

During the Sikh holiday known as Vaisakhi, the founding of the Khalsa sect is remembered (sometimes written Baisakhi). Every year on April 14th, it is observed with parades, music, and dancing.

Other festivals and traditions

The first day of the year, January 1, is a holiday. On December 31, commonly known as New Year's Eve, people typically enjoy themselves. Scotland declares December 31 a public holiday in observance of Hogmanay. Some Scots consider Hogmanay to be more important than Christmas.

The day of Valentine's Day, February 14, is marked by card and gift exchanges. People occasionally send cards to people they secretly admire.

People joke around with one another until noon on April 1. Newspaper and broadcast reports commonly contain April Fool's Day pranks.

Mothering Sunday, also known as Mother's Day, falls on the Sunday before Easter. Children can mail cards or presents to their mothers.

The third Sunday in June is Father's Day. For their fathers, kids can purchase presents or cards.

Bank holidays

Bank holidays in the UK are public holidays designated by the UK government. They are days when most businesses and non-essential services are closed, and employees are entitled to a day off work or extra pay for working on these days.

In England, Wales, and Northern Ireland, there are eight bank holidays each year, while Scotland has nine. The dates of bank holidays can vary slightly each year, but the following are the usual dates:

New Year's Day - January 1st

Good Friday - the Friday before Easter Sunday

Easter Monday - the Monday after Easter Sunday

Early May Bank Holiday - first Monday in May

Spring Bank Holiday - last Monday in May

Summer Bank Holiday - last Monday in August

Christmas Day - December 25th

Boxing Day - December 26th

In Scotland, an additional bank holiday is observed on January 2nd, known as the "2nd January holiday" or "New Year's Day (2nd of January)"; and there is an additional bank holiday in England, Wales and Northern Ireland on December 27th, known as the "Boxing Day (substitute day)".

It's important to note that bank holidays may affect the opening times of shops, banks, and other services, and public transport may operate on a reduced schedule.

Cricket

In the United Kingdom, cricket is a well-liked sport, and the nation has a long history with it. The first formal international cricket match was played between England and Australia in 1877, and the first cricket match in England was first noted in the 16th century.

The County Championship, the highest level of domestic cricket in England and Wales, as well as the T20 Blast and the Royal London One-Day Cup are just a few of the domestic cricket competitions held in the UK.

One of the best teams in the world, the England cricket team represents the nation internationally. They have finished in second place three times and have only ever won the ICC Cricket World Cup once, in 2019. The team also participates frequently in the Ashes series, one of cricket's most illustrious and historic rivalries versus Australia.

Overall, cricket is still a well-liked and often played sport in the UK, and many people take pleasure in both watching and participating in the game.

Football

In the United Kingdom, football (sometimes referred to as soccer) is a hugely popular sport (UK). Millions of people of different ages, genders, and backgrounds play the game, which has a long history in the UK. With many people passionately and loyally supporting their local and national teams, it is also a significant component of UK culture and identity.

The Premier League, the Championship, League One, and League Two are the four professional football leagues in the UK. The Premier League, the top division, is renowned as one of the world's premier football leagues. The EFL refers to the three leagues that come after the Premier League (English Football League). The Scottish Premiership is a professional football league that exists in Scotland.

Numerous well-known football teams, including Manchester United, Liverpool, Arsenal, Chelsea, and Tottenham Hotspur, are based in the UK. These teams are among the most prosperous and well-known football teams in the world, and they have a sizable international fan base.

But professional leagues and teams are not the only things that matter in British football. Along with recreational leagues for players of all ages and skill levels, the nation is home to a large number of amateur and semi-professional leagues and teams. Anyone can love football, and it plays a significant role in local culture throughout much of the UK.

The UEFA Euro 1996, the 2012 Summer Olympics, and some of the biggest football tournaments in the history of the game have all taken place in the UK. These occasions have increased tourism to the UK and strengthened the nation's standing as a footballing powerhouse.

Rugby

In the UK, rugby is a well-liked sport with a lengthy and fascinating history. Rugby was invented in England in the nineteenth century, and it has since gained popularity throughout the UK and the rest of the world.

In the UK, rugby is played in a variety of ways, including Rugby Union and Rugby League. The more well-known of the two sports, rugby union, is played on both the amateur and professional levels. It is a well-liked sport in Scotland, Ireland, and England. It is the national sport of Wales. One of the most renowned rugby competitions in the world, the Six Nations Championship, which is played between England, Scotland, Wales, Ireland, France, and Italy, is very popular among rugby fans.

In the north of England, rugby league is more widely played at both the amateur and professional levels. Rugby league clubs from France, Wales, and England compete in the Super League, the highest tier of rugby league sport in the UK.

Over the years, the UK has produced numerous outstanding rugby players, including Gareth Edwards, Martin Johnson, Jason Robinson, and Jonny Wilkinson, among others. The activity continues to pique the interest of both players and spectators, and it plays a significant role in British sporting culture.

Horse-racing

In Britain, where horse racing has a lengthy history, records of races date all the way back to the Roman era. The sport has traditionally been connected to the nobility. In the UK, there are many racetracks. The Scottish Grand National at Ayr, the Grand National at Aintree, close to Liverpool, and the five-day Royal Ascot race meeting in Berkshire, which is attended by members of the Royal Family, are all well-known horse racing occasions. In Newmarket, Suffolk, there is a National Horseracing Museum.

Golf

The United Kingdom has a long history with golf, and many people consider it to be where the game first originated. Some of the most famous golf courses in the world, including St. Andrews, Royal Birkdale, Royal Troon, Muirfield, and Royal St. George's, are located in the UK.

Golf can be enjoyed in the UK in a variety of ways, from playing on public courses to joining exclusive clubs. Golf is much-liked across the nation, and many neighborhood clubs provide memberships at reasonable prices as well as chances for both competitive and recreational play.

A number of significant golf competitions are also staged in the UK, including The Open Championship, one of the four major tournaments in professional golf. It is contested yearly at one of the best courses in the nation.

There are numerous tools at your disposal to assist you in making your travel itinerary if you're organizing a golf trip to the UK. There are tour companies that specialize in golf trips, and you can study courses and make tee time reservations online as well. Just be aware that some of the best restaurants may have tight dress regulations and advance reservations, so it's wise to verify the policies before you go.

Tennis

Tennis has a long and illustrious history in the UK that dates back to the 19th century. Wimbledon, the most well-known competition in the sport, is held yearly in London and is recognized as the most prestigious tennis competition in the world.

The Lawn Tennis Association (LTA), which serves as the sport's regulating organization in the UK, is in charge of growing tennis there. The LTA seeks to promote tennis involvement among people of all ages and skill levels, from recreational play to elite competition.

In the UK, there are several tennis clubs and facilities, many of which offer teaching and training courses for players of various skill levels. The Queen's Club Championships and the ATP Finals are just two of the professional tennis competitions that are held in the UK in addition to Wimbledon.

Over the years, British tennis has produced some noteworthy athletes, including as Andy Murray, Tim Henman, Virginia Wade, and Fred Perry. Particularly Murray, who recently won an Olympic gold medal and many Grand Slam championships, has seen enormous success.

Motor sports

The United Kingdom has a long and illustrious history in motor sports, with a wide range of competitions and disciplines held there. In the UK, some of the most well-liked motorsports are:

Formula One: The most successful and well-known Formula One teams, including as Mercedes, Red Bull, and Williams, are based in the UK. The British Grand Prix, which takes place yearly at the Silverstone Circuit, is one of the most prominent events on the F1 calendar.

MotoGP: Motorcycle racing is a popular sport in the UK, and the Silverstone Circuit hosts the British MotoGP.

Rallying: Rallying is a type of motorsport that involves competing on off-road or closed-to-the-public roads. Top drivers and teams from all over the world compete in the Wales Rally GB, a prominent event on the World Rally Championship schedule.

Touring cars: The British Touring Car Championship is the most well-known series of racing in the touring car category in the UK. Honda, BMW, and Ford are just a few of the manufacturers and models competing in the competition.

Karting is a well-liked kind of motorsport for both kids and adults, and there are both indoor and outdoor karting circuits spread out over the UK.

In addition to these competitions, the UK has a variety of other motorsport competitions, such as oval racing, drag racing, and hill climbs. The UK is also the birthplace of several well-known drivers, teams, and tracks, giving the nation a rich motorsports tradition.

Arts and culture

Theatre

Theatre is an important part of the cultural landscape in the United Kingdom. The UK has a rich theatrical tradition, with a long history of producing world-class plays and performances. Here are some key things to know about theatre in the UK:

West End: The West End is London's main theatre district and is home to many of the city's most famous theatres, including the Apollo, the Lyceum, the Palladium, and the Royal Opera House. The West End is known for its large-scale productions of popular musicals and plays, as well as its more experimental and avant-garde shows.

Fringe Theatre: In addition to the West End, the UK has a thriving fringe theatre scene. Fringe theatre is typically smaller, more experimental, and less commercial than West End productions. Fringe shows can be found throughout the country, but are particularly prominent in London and Edinburgh.

National Theatre: The National Theatre is one of the UK's most prestigious theatres and is based in London. It is known for producing high-quality productions of classic plays and new works by contemporary writers.

Shakespeare: William Shakespeare is widely regarded as one of the greatest playwrights in history, and his plays are still performed regularly in the UK and around the world. The Globe Theatre in London is a replica of the theatre where many of Shakespeare's plays were first performed.

Pantomime: Pantomime is a traditional form of theatre that is popular in the UK, particularly around the Christmas season. Pantomime shows are typically family-friendly productions that include elements of comedy, music, dance, and audience participation.

Diversity: Theatre in the UK has become increasingly diverse in recent years, with more productions featuring actors and performers from a wide range of backgrounds. There has also been a growing focus on promoting diversity in the industry, both on and off stage.

Art

The UK is home to some of the most renowned art institutions and artists in the world and has a long history of artistic production. The UK boasts a lively art scene with a varied spectrum of styles and genres, from traditional to modern art.

The Tate, which consists of the four galleries Tate Britain, Tate Modern, Tate Liverpool, and Tate St. Ives, is one of the most well-known art institutions in the UK. A wide variety of modern and contemporary works are on display at these galleries, in addition to pieces from the UK's historical art canon. Another well-known museum of art with a collection of Western European paintings from the 13th to the 19th centuries is London's National Gallery.

The UK also includes a variety of smaller, independent galleries that feature up-and-coming and established artists in addition to the larger art museums. With numerous galleries and art fairs spread out over the city, London is a particularly active center for the arts. The art scenes in other places including Glasgow, Edinburgh, and Manchester are also prospering.

Famous artists including J.M.W. Turner, John Constable, Francis Bacon, and David Hockney were all born in the UK. Additionally, contemporary artists like Tracey Emin, Damien Hirst, and Banksy have achieved success on a global scale.

Fashion and design

Sir Terence Conran, Clarice Cliff, and Thomas Chippendale are just a few of the well-known designers that came from Britain. The 18th century saw the creation of furniture by Thomas Chippendale (a 20th-century interior designer). Vivienne Westwood, Mary Quant, and Alexander McQueen are some of the top fashion designers from recent years.

Literature

The UK has a distinguished literary heritage. A number of British authors, including playwright Harold Pinter, poet Seamus Heaney, and novelist Sir William Golding, have won the Nobel Prize for Literature. Popular fiction has produced several well-known authors. The world reads Agatha Christie's detective novels, and Ian Fleming's James Bond novels introduced the character. JRR Tolkien's The Lord of the Rings was chosen as the nation's favorite book in 2003.

Each year, the Commonwealth, Ireland, or Zimbabwe author of the best fiction novel receives the Man Booker Prize for Fiction. Since 1968, it has been presented. Previous winners include Julian Barnes, Hilary Mantel, and Ian McEwan.

Chapter 4:
UK Government, The Laws, And Main Principles

The UK is a parliamentary democracy with the monarch as head of state. This section will tell you about the different institutions which make up this democratic system and explain how you can play a part in the democratic process.

The development of British democracy

Democracy is a system of government where the whole adult population gets a say. This might be by direct voting or by choosing representatives to make decisions on their behalf.

At the turn of the 19th century, Britain was not a democracy as we know it today. Although there were elections to select members of Parliament (MPs), only a small group of people could vote. They were men who were over 21 years of age and who owned a certain amount of property.

The franchise (that is, the number of people who had the right to vote) grew over the course of the 19th century and political parties began to involve ordinary men and women as members.

In the 1830s and 1840s, a group called the Chartists campaigned for reform. They wanted six changes:

- for every man to have the vote
- elections every year
- for all regions to be equal in the electoral system
- secret ballots
- for any man to be able to stand as an MP
- for MPs to be paid.

At the time, the campaign was generally seen as a failure. However, by 1918 most of these reforms had been adopted. The voting franchise was also extended to women over 30, and then in 1928 to men and women over 21. In 1969, the voting age was reduced to 18 for men and women.

The British constitution

A constitution is a set of guiding ideas that determines how a nation is run. It covers every entity in charge of leading the nation and how their authority is restrained. Laws and conventions are also included in the constitution. The British constitution is said to as "unwritten" since it is not included in a single document. This is mostly due to the fact that, unlike America or France, the UK has never seen a revolution that resulted in a wholly new form of government that lasted forever. Our most significant institutions have evolved over many centuries. Some people think the constitution should just be one document, while others think an unwritten constitution provides for better government and more flexibility.

Constitutional institutions

In the UK, there are several different parts of government. The main ones are:

- the monarchy
- Parliament (the House of Commons and the House of Lords)
- the Prime Minister
- the cabinet
- the judiciary (courts)
- the police
- the civil service
- local government.

In addition, there are devolved governments in Scotland, Wales and Northern Ireland that have the power to legislate on certain issues.

The monarchy

The UK's current head of state is Queen Elizabeth II. She also serves as the queen or head of state for numerous Commonwealth nations. The monarchy in the UK is constitutional. In other words, the government, which the people have elected in a democratic election, is appointed by the monarch or queen rather than ruling the nation. The head of the party with the most representatives in parliament or the head of a coalition made up of several parties receives an invitation from the king to serve as prime minister. The queen meets with the prime minister on a regular basis and is able to give advice, issue warnings, and offer encouragement, but the prime minister and cabinet are the ones who decide on government policies.

Queen Elizabeth II

The Queen has been in power since her father died in 1952, and she commemorated her Diamond Jubilee in 2012. (60 years as queen). Prince Philip, the Duke of Edinburgh, is her husband. The heir to the throne is her oldest son, Prince Charles (the Prince of Wales).

The Queen performs significant ceremonial duties, such as officiating at the beginning of each new legislative session. The Queen speaks on this occasion and outlines the government's plans for the coming year. She is the author of all Acts of Parliament.

To the rest of the world, the UK is represented by the Queen. In order to strengthen diplomatic and commercial ties with other nations, she hosts visiting heads of state, greets foreign ambassadors and high commissioners, and undertakes state visits abroad.

The Queen plays a crucial part in ensuring consistency and stability. The Queen continues to serve as head of state even though administrations and Prime Ministers frequently change. She serves as a focal point for national pride, which was evident during the Jubilee celebrations.

The national anthem

The National Anthem of the UK is 'God Save the Queen'. It is played at important national occasions and at events attended by the Queen or the Royal Family. The first verse is:

'God save our gracious Queen!

Long live our noble Queen!

God save the Queen!

Send her victorious,

Happy and glorious,

Long to reign over us,

God save the Queen!'

New citizens swear or affirm loyalty to the Queen as part of the citizenship ceremony.

Oath of allegiance

'I (name) swear by Almighty God that on becoming a British citizen, I will be faithful and bear true allegiance to Her Majesty Queen Elizabeth the Second, her Heirs and Successors, according to law.'

Affirmation of allegiance

'I (name) do solemnly, sincerely and truly declare and affirm that on becoming a British citizen, I will be faithful and bear true allegiance to Her Majesty Queen Elizabeth the Second, her Heirs and Successors, according to law.'

System of government

The system of government in the UK is a parliamentary democracy. The UK is divided into parliamentary constituencies. Voters in each constituency elect their member of Parliament (MP) in a General Election. All of the elected MPs form the House of Commons. Most MPs belong to a political party, and the party with the majority of MPs forms the government. If one party does not get a majority, two parties can join together to form a coalition.

The Parliament in Westminster

The House of Commons

The House of Commons is regarded as the more important of the two chambers in Parliament because its members are democratically elected. The Prime Minister and almost all the members of the cabinet are members of the House of Commons (MPs). Each MP represents a parliamentary constituency, which is a small area of the country. MPs have a number of different responsibilities. They:

- represent everyone in their constituency
- help to create new laws
- scrutinize and comment on what the government is doing.
- debate important national issues.

The House of Lords

Members of the House of Lords, known as peers, are not elected by the people and do not represent a constituency. The role and membership of the House of Lords has changed over the last 50 years.

Until 1958, all peers were:

- 'hereditary', which means they inherited their title, or
- senior judges, or
- bishops of the Church of England.

Since 1958, the Prime Minister has had the power to nominate peers just for their own lifetime. These are called life peers. They have usually had an important career in politics, business, law or another profession. Life peers are appointed by the monarch on the advice of the Prime Minister. They also include people nominated by the leaders of the other main political parties or by an independent Appointments Commission for non-party peers.

Since 1999, hereditary peers have lost the automatic right to attend the House of Lords. They now elect a few of their number to represent them in the House of Lords.

The House of Lords is normally more independent of the government than the House of Commons. It can suggest amendments or propose new laws, which are then discussed by MPs. The House of Lords checks laws that have been passed by the House of Commons to ensure they are fit for purpose. It also holds the government to account to make sure that it is working in the best interests of the people. There are peers who are specialists in particular areas, and their knowledge is useful in making and checking laws. The House of Commons has powers to overrule the House of Lords, but these are not used often.

The Speaker

Debates in the House of Commons are chaired by the Speaker. This person is the chief officer of the House of Commons. The Speaker is neutral and does not represent a political party, even though he or she is an MP, represents a constituency and deals with constituents' problems like any other MP. The Speaker is chosen by other MPs in a secret ballot.

The Speaker keeps order during political debates to make sure the rules are followed. This includes making sure the opposition (see the section on 'The government') has a guaranteed amount of time to debate issues which it chooses. The Speaker also represents Parliament on ceremonial occasions.

Elections

UK elections

MPs are elected at a General Election, which is held at least every five years.

If an MP dies or resigns, there will be a fresh election, called a by-election, in his or her constituency.

MPs are elected through a system called 'first past the post'. In each constituency, the candidate who gets the most votes is elected. The government is usually formed by the party that wins the majority of constituencies. If no party wins a majority, two parties may join together to form a coalition.

Contacting elected members

All elected members have a duty to serve and represent their constituents. You can get contact details for all your representatives and their parties from your local library and from www.parliament.uk. MPs, Assembly members and members of the Scottish Parliament (MSPs) are also listed in The Phone Book, published by BT.

You can contact MPs by letter or telephone at their constituency office, or at their office in the House of Commons: The House of Commons, Westminster, London SW1A 0AA, telephone 020 7129 3000. In addition, many MPs, Assembly members and MSPs hold regular local 'surgeries', where constituents can go in person to talk about issues that are of concern to them. These surgeries are often advertised in the local newspaper.

Check that you understand:

- How democracy has developed in the UK
- What a constitution is and how the UK's constitution is different from those of most other countries
- The role of the monarch
- The role of the House of Commons and House of Lords
- What the Speaker does
- How the UK elects MPs and MEPs
- The government

The Prime Minister

The Prime Minister (PM) is the leader of the political party in power. He or she appoints the members of the cabinet (see below) and has control over many important public appointments. The official home of the Prime Minister is 10 Downing Street, in central London, near the Houses of Parliament. He or she also has a country house outside London called Chequers.

The Prime Minister can be changed if the MPs in the governing party decide to do so, or if he or she wishes to resign. The Prime Minister usually resigns if his or her party loses a General Election.

The cabinet

The Prime Minister appoints about 20 senior MPs to become ministers in charge of departments. These include:

- Chancellor of the Exchequer – responsible for the economy
- Home Secretary – responsible for crime, policing and immigration
- Foreign Secretary – responsible for managing relationships with foreign countries
- other ministers (called 'Secretaries of State') responsible for subjects such as education, health and defence.

These ministers form the cabinet, a committee which usually meets weekly and makes important decisions about government policy. Many of these decisions have to be debated or approved by Parliament.

Each department also has a number of other ministers, called Ministers of State and Parliamentary Under-Secretaries of State, who take charge of particular areas of the department's work.

The opposition

The second-largest party in the House of Commons is called the opposition. The leader of the opposition usually becomes Prime Minister if his or her party wins the next General Election.

The leader of the opposition leads his or her party in pointing out what they see as the government's failures and weaknesses. One important opportunity to do this is at Prime Minister's Questions, which takes place every week while Parliament is sitting. The leader of the opposition also appoints senior opposition MPs to be 'shadow ministers'. They form the shadow cabinet and their role is to challenge the government and put forward alternative policies.

The party system

Anyone aged 18 or over can stand for election as an MP but they are unlikely to win unless they have been nominated to represent one of the major political parties. These are the Conservative Party, the Labour Party, the Liberal Democrats, or one of the parties representing Scottish, Welsh or Northern Irish interests.

There are a few MPs who do not represent any of the main political parties. They are called 'independents' and usually represent an issue important to their constituency.

The main political parties actively look for members of the public to join their debates, contribute to their costs, and help at elections for Parliament or for local government. They have branches in most constituencies and hold policy-making conferences every year.

Pressure and lobby groups are organisations which try to influence government policy. They play an important role in politics. Some are representative organisations such as the CBI (Confederation of British Industry), which represents the views of British business. Others campaign on particular topics, such as the environment (for example, Greenpeace) or human rights (for example, Liberty).

The civil service

Civil servants support the government in developing and implementing its policies. They also deliver public services. Civil servants are accountable to ministers. They are chosen on merit and are politically neutral – they are not political appointees. People can apply to join the civil service through an application process, like other jobs in the UK. Civil servants are expected to carry out their role with dedication and a commitment to the civil service and its core values. These are: integrity, honesty, objectivity and impartiality (including being politically neutral).

Local government

Towns, cities and rural areas in the UK are governed by democratically elected councils, often called 'local authorities'. Some areas have both district and county councils, which have different functions. Most large towns and cities have a single local authority.

Local authorities provide a range of services in their areas. They are funded by money from central government and by local taxes.

Many local authorities appoint a mayor, who is the ceremonial leader of the council. In some towns, a mayor is elected to be the effective leader of the administration. London has 33 local authorities, with the Greater London Authority and the Mayor of London coordinating policies across the capital. For most local authorities, local elections for councillors are held in May every year. Many candidates stand for council election as members of a political party.

Devolved administrations.

Since 1997, some powers have been devolved from the central government to give people in Wales, Scotland and Northern Ireland more control over matters that directly affect them.

There has been a Welsh Assembly and a Scottish Parliament since 1999. There is also a Northern Ireland Assembly, although this has been suspended on a few occasions.

Policy and laws governing defence, foreign affairs, immigration, taxation and social security all remain under central UK government control. However, many other public services, such as education, are controlled by the devolved administrations.

The devolved administrations each have their own civil service.

The Welsh government

The Welsh government and National Assembly for Wales are based in Cardiff, the capital city of Wales. The National Assembly has 60 Assembly members (AMs) and elections are held every four years using a form of proportional representation. Members can speak in either Welsh or English, and all of the Assembly's publications are in both languages.

Senedd, Welsh parliament

The Assembly has the power to make laws for Wales in 21 areas, including:

- education and training
- health and social services
- economic development
- housing.

Since 2011, the National Assembly for Wales has been able to pass laws on these topics without the agreement of the UK Parliament.

The Scottish Parliament

The Scottish Parliament was formed in 1999. It sits in Edinburgh, the capital city of Scotland.

Public entrance of the Scottish Parliament building

There are 129 members of the Scottish Parliament (MSPs), elected by a form of proportional representation. The Scottish Parliament can pass laws for Scotland on all matters which are not specifically reserved to the UK Parliament. The matters on which the Scottish Parliament can legislate include:

civil and criminal law

- health
- education
- planning
- additional tax-raising powers.

The Northern Ireland Assembly

A Northern Ireland Parliament was established in 1922, when Ireland was divided, but it was abolished in 1972, shortly after the Troubles broke out in 1969.

The Northern Ireland Assembly was established soon after the Belfast Agreement (or Good Friday Agreement) in 1998. There is a power-sharing agreement which distributes ministerial offices amongst the main parties. The Assembly has 108 elected members, known as MLAs (members of the Legislative Assembly). They are elected with a form of proportional representation.

The Northern Ireland Assembly can make decisions on issues such as:

- education
- agriculture
- the environment
- health

- social services.

The UK government has the power to suspend all devolved assemblies. It has used this power several times in Northern Ireland when local political leaders found it difficult to work together. However, the Assembly has been running successfully since 2007.

The media and government

Proceedings in Parliament are broadcast on television and published in official reports called Hansard. Written reports can be found in large libraries and at www.parliament.uk. Most people get information about political issues and events from newspapers (often called 'the press'), television, radio and the internet.

The UK has a free press. This means that what is written in newspapers is free from government control. Some newspaper owners and editors hold strong political opinions and run campaigns to try to influence government policy and public opinion.

By law, radio and television coverage of the political parties must be balanced and so equal time has to be given to rival viewpoints.

Check that you understand:

- The role of the Prime Minister, cabinet, opposition and shadow cabinet
- The role of political parties in the UK system of government
- Who the main political parties are
- What pressure and lobby groups do
- The role of the civil service
- The role of local government
- The powers of the devolved governments in Wales, Scotland and Northern Ireland
- How proceedings in Parliament are recorded

- The role of the media in keeping people informed about political issues

Who can vote?

The UK has had a fully democratic voting system since 1928. The present voting age of 18 was set in 1969 and (with a few exceptions) all UK-born and naturalised adult citizens have the right to vote.

Adult citizens of the UK, and citizens of the Commonwealth and Ireland who are resident in the UK, can vote in all public elections. Adult citizens of other EU states who are resident in the UK can vote in all elections except General Elections.

The electoral register

To be able to vote in a parliamentary, local or European election, you must have your name on the electoral register.

If you are eligible to vote, you can register by contacting your local council electoral registration office. This is usually based at your local council (in Scotland it may be based elsewhere). If you don't know which local authority you come under, you can find out by visiting www.aboutmyvote.co.uk and entering your postcode. You can also download voter registration forms in English, Welsh and some other languages.

The electoral register is updated every year in September or October. An electoral registration form is sent to every household and this has to be completed and returned with the names of everyone who is resident in the household and eligible to vote.

In Northern Ireland a different system operates. This is called 'individual registration' and all those entitled to vote must complete their own registration form. Once registered, people stay on the register provided their personal details do not change. For more information see the Electoral Office for Northern Ireland website at www.eoni.org.uk.

By law, each local authority has to make its electoral register available for anyone to look at, although this has to be supervised. The register is kept at each local electoral registration office (or council office in England and Wales). It is also possible to see the register at some public buildings such as libraries.

Where to vote

People vote in elections at places called polling stations, or polling places in Scotland. Before the election you will be sent a poll card. This tells you where your polling station or polling place is and when the election will take place. On election day, the polling station or place will be open from 7.00 am until 10.00 pm.

When you arrive at the polling station, the staff will ask for your name and address. In Northern Ireland you will also have to show photographic identification. You will then get your ballot paper, which you take to a polling booth to fill in privately. You should make up your own mind who to vote for. No one has the right to make you vote for a particular candidate. You should follow the instructions on the ballot paper. Once you have completed it, put it in the ballot box.

If it is difficult for you to get to a polling station or polling place, you can register for a postal ballot. Your ballot paper will be sent to your home before the election. You then fill it in and post it back. You can choose to do this when you register to vote.

Standing for office

Most citizens of the UK, Ireland or the Commonwealth aged 18 or over can stand for public office. There are some exceptions, including:

- members of the armed forces
- civil servants

- people found guilty of certain criminal offences.

Members of the House of Lords may not stand for election to the House of Commons but are eligible for all other public offices.

Visiting Parliament and the devolved administrations

The UK Parliament

The public can listen to debates in the Palace of Westminster from public galleries in both the House of Commons and the House of Lords.

You can write to your local MP in advance to ask for tickets or you can queue on the day at the public entrance. Entrance is free. Sometimes there are long queues for the House of Commons and people have to wait for at least one or two hours. It is usually easier to get into the House of Lords.

Chapter 5:
The Process Of Becoming A Citizen Or Permanent Resident

Becoming a permanent resident

To apply to become a permanent resident or naturalized citizen of the UK, you will need to:

- speak and read English.
- have a good understanding of life in the UK.

This means you will need to:

- Pass the Life in the UK Test

AND

- Produce acceptable evidence of speaking and listening skills in English at B1 of the Common European Framework of Reference. This is equivalent to ESOL Entry Level 3. There is a wide range of qualifications or ways that may be used to demonstrate this. Some of these test speaking and listening skills only. Others also test reading and writing skills. You will be able to choose a qualification that suits your requirements. For further details on how to demonstrate evidence of the required level of speaking and listening skills in English, please visit the Home Office website.

It is possible that the requirements may change in the future. You should check the information on the Home Office website for current requirements before applying for settlement or citizenship.

Taking the Life in the UK Test

This handbook will help prepare you for taking the Life in the UK Test. The test consists of 24 questions about important aspects of life in the UK. Questions are based on ALL parts of the handbook. The 24 questions will be different for each person taking the test at that test session.

The Life in the UK Test is usually taken in English, although special arrangements can be made if you wish to take it in Welsh or Scottish Gaelic.

You can only take the test at a registered and approved Life in the UK Test center. There are about 60 test centers around the UK. You can only book your test online, at www.lifeintheuktest.gov.uk. You should not take your test at any other establishment as the Home Office will only accept certificates from registered test centers. If you live on the Isle of Man or in the Channel Islands, there are different arrangements for taking the Life in the UK Test.

When booking your test, read the instructions carefully. Make sure you enter your details correctly. You will need to take some identification and proof of your address with you to the test. If you don't take these, you will not be able to take the test.

Do you want to become a citizen of the United Kingdom? It is possible, but first you need to know how this process works. This post will help you understand what steps you need to take in order to become a UK citizen or permanent resident.

British Citizenship Through Ancestry

If you are eligible for UK citizenship through ancestry then this is by far one of the most common ways for people to get citizenship. The process will require you to first take a test in order to demonstrate proficiency in English and knowledge about English history, law and government (civics). In addition, you will take a test to demonstrate knowledge of the UK's current affairs and political structure.

The good news is that there are many resources to help you study for these tests. One of the best, and most popular options, would be to get official practice tests from the government site, gov.uk . There are also many other websites where students of English can find more information about citizenship.

While you are taking the citizenship test, there are a couple of things to consider. First, you will want to make sure that you fully understand what you need to do in order to pass the test. The easiest way to determine this is by taking a course that teaches English language basics.

Furthermore, it is important that you request legal representation through your local British consulate or Embassy if you are taking this test. You may be able to count on the embassy or consulate for help with the test.

Once you have passed your citizenship test, it is time to get the necessary documents and paperwork. The application process will require you to submit several forms, including three documents to prove that you are British at least through a parent (birth certificate), marriage certificate, and proof of employment (a letter from your employer). The final step is to send in your passport, a photocopied portion of your birth certificate, and a copy of the citizenship test result. If you are living outside the UK, you will need to present all of these documents to your local British embassy or consulate.

Your application will then be sent off to the Home Office for processing. You will receive a letter confirming that your application has been accepted and an appointment time for an interview at which point it will all be confirmed and you can finally take the oath of

British Citizenship Through Marriage

British citizenship through marriage to a UK citizen, or permanent resident, is another way in which you can become a citizen. Eligibility for this type of citizenship will require you to be married for at least two years. In addition, the UK citizen or permanent resident that you are marrying must be at least 18 years of age (21+ with written consent). There are some requirements for residency as well if your spouse is not already a British citizen.

The process for this is relatively simple. If you are outside of the UK, you will need to present your marriage certificate, a photocopy of both partners' passports, proof of address in the UK for at least 2 years, and proof of employment (a letter from your employer). It is important to note that if the spouse you are marrying is already a permanent resident, there are fewer requirements.

If you are living in the UK and have been married for more than one year, it is possible to go through a faster process to become a citizen. This process requires you to fill out an application form, provide proof of address and employment (as well as confirmation from your bank), and send in your current marriage certificate. In addition, you will need to provide the Home Office with a copy of the birth certificate of your spouse as well as a copy of their British passport.

Once your citizenship application has been approved, you will be contacted by an immigration official and scheduled an appointment time. At this point, you will need to take an oath of allegiance to the queen, be fingerprinted and photographed, and collect your Certificate confirming you are now a British citizen.

Chapter 6:
Getting Involved In Your Community

Becoming a British Citizen or settling in the UK brings responsibilities but also opportunities. Everyone has the opportunity to participate in their community. This section looks at some of the responsibilities of being a citizen and gives information about how you can help to make your community a better place to live and work.

Values and responsibilities

Although Britain is one of the world's most diverse societies, there is a set of shared values and responsibilities that everyone can agree with. These values and responsibilities include:

- To obey and respect the law
- To be aware of the rights of others and respect those rights
- To treat others with fairness
- To behave responsibly

- To help and protect your family
- To respect and preserve the environment
- To treat everyone equally, regardless of sex, race, religion, age, disability, class or sexual orientation
- To work to provide for yourself and your family
- To help others
- To vote in local and national government elections

Taking on these values and responsibilities will make it easier for you to become a full and active citizen.

Being a good neighbor

When you move into a new house or apartment, introduce yourself to the people who live near you. Getting to know your neighbors can help you to become part of the community and make friends. Your neighbors are also a good source of help – for example, they may be willing to feed your pets if you are away, or offer advice on local shops and services.

You can help prevent any problems and conflicts with your neighbors by respecting their privacy and limiting how much noise you make. Also try to keep your garden tidy, and only put your refuse bags and bins on the street or in communal areas if they are due to be collected.

Getting involved in local activities.

Volunteering and helping your community are an important part of being a good citizen. They enable you to integrate with other people. It helps make your community a better place if residents support each other. It also helps you to fulfill your duties a citizen, such as behaving responsibly and helping others.

HOW YOU CAN SUPPORT YOUR COMMUNITY

There are a number of positive ways in which you can support your community and be a good citizen.

1. Jury service

As well as getting the right to vote, people on the electoral role are randomly selected to serve on a jury. Anyone who is on the electoral register and is aged 18 to 70 can be asked to do this.

2. Helping in schools

If you have children, there are many ways in which you can help at their schools. Parents can often help in classrooms, by supporting activities or listening to children read.

Many schools organize events to raise money for extra equipment or out-of-school activities. Activities might include book sales, toy sales or bringing food to sell. You might have good ideas of your own for raising money. Sometimes events are organized by parent-teacher associations (PTAs). Volunteering to help with their events or joining the association is a way of doing something good for the school and also making new friends in your local community. You can find out about these opportunities from notices in the school or notes your children bring home.

3. School governors and school boards

School governors, or members of the school board in Scotland, are people from the local community who wish to make a positive contribution to children's education. They must be 18 or over at the date of their election or appointment. There is no upper age limit.

Governors and school boards have an important part to play in raising school standards. They have three key roles:

1. Setting the strategic direction of the school
2. Ensuring accountability
3. Monitoring and evaluating school performance.

You can contact your local school to ask if they need a new governor or school board member. In England, you can also apply online at the School Governors' One

In England, parents and other community groups can apply to open a free school in their local area. More information about this can be found on the Department.

Supporting political parties

Political parties' welcome new members. Joining one is a way to demonstrate your support for certain views and to get involved in the democratic process.

Political parties are particularly busy at election times. Members work hard to persuade people to vote for their candidates – for instance, by handing out leaflets in the street or by knocking on people's doors and asking for their support. This is called 'canvassing'. You don't have to tell a canvasser how you intend to vote if you don't want to.

British citizens stand for office as a local councilor, a member of Parliament (or the devolved equivalents) or a member of the European Parliament. This is an opportunity to become even more involved in political life in the UK. You may also be able to stand for office if you are an Irish citizen, an eligible Commonwealth citizen or (except for standing as an MP) a citizen of another European country. You can find out more about joining a political party from the individual party websites.

Helping with local services

There are opportunities to volunteer with a wide range of local service providers, including local hospitals and youth projects. Services often want to involve local people in decisions about the way they work. Universities, housing associations, museums and arts councils may advertise for people to serve as volunteers in their governing bodies.

You can volunteer with the police and become a special constable or a lay (non-police) representative. You can also apply to become a magistrate. You will find advertisements for vacancies in your local newspaper or on local radio.

Other ways to volunteer

Volunteering is working for good causes without payment. There are many benefits to volunteering, such as meeting new people and helping make your community a better place. Some volunteer activities will give you a chance to practice your English or develop work skills that will help you find a job or improve your curriculum vitae (CV). Many people volunteer simply because they want to help other people.

Activities you can do as a volunteer include:

- Working with animals – for example, caring for animals at a local rescue shelter
- Youth work – for example, volunteering at a youth group
- Helping to improve the environment – for example, participating in a litter pick-up in the local area
- Working with the homeless in, for example, a homelessness shelter
- Mentoring – for example, supporting someone who has just come out of prison
- Work in health and hospitals – for example, working on an information desk in an hospital
- Helping older people at, for example, a residential care home

There are thousands of active charities and voluntary organisations in the UK. They work to improve the lives of people, animals and the environment in many different ways. They range from the British branches of international organisations, such as the British Red Cross, to small local charities working in particular areas. They include charities working with older people (such as Age UK), with children (for example, the National Society for the Prevention of Cruelty to Children (NSPCC)), and with the homeless (for example, Crisis and Shelter). There are also medical research charities (for example, Cancer Research UK), environmental charities (including the National Trust and Friends of the Earth) and charities working with animals (such as the People's Dispensary for Sick Animals (PDSA)).

Volunteers are needed to help with their activities and to raise money. The charities often advertise in local newspapers, and most have websites that include information about their opportunities.

There are many opportunities for younger people to volunteer and receive accreditation which will help them to develop their skills. These include the National Citizen Service program, which gives 16- and 17-year olds the opportunity to enjoy outdoor activities, develop their skills and take part in a community project.

LOOKING AFTER THE ENVIRONMENT

It is important to recycle as much of your waste as you can. Using recycled materials to make new products uses less energy and means that we do not need to extract more raw materials from the earth. It also means that less rubbish is created, so the amount being put into landfill is reduced.

A good way to support your local community is to shop for products locally where you can. This will help businesses and farmers in your area and in Britain. It will also reduce your carbon footprint because the products you buy will not have travelled so far.

Walking and using public transport to get around when you can is also a good way to protect the environment. It means that you create less pollution than when you use a car.

Check that you understand

- The different ways you can help at your child's school
- The role of school governors and members of school boards and how you become one
- The role of members of political parties
- The different local services people can volunteer to support
- How to donate blood and organs
- The benefits of volunteering for you, other people and the community
- The types of activities that volunteers can do
- How you can look after the environment

Chapter 7:
How The Test To Get The UK Citizenship Works

You must pass the Life in the UK test and fulfill the residency requirements in order to become a citizen of the United Kingdom. The purpose of the test is to gauge your familiarity with British history, culture, and customs.

Here is a description of the test's methodology:

To be eligible to take the test, you must be at least 18 years old and have lived in the UK legally for at least five years.

Test scheduling: The official government website allows you to schedule the test either over the phone or online. The exam is £50 in price.

There are 24 multiple-choice questions on the test, and you have 45 minutes to do it. These include British history, governance, legislation, and customs, among other subjects.

You must correctly respond to at least 18 out of the test's 24 questions in order to pass (75 percent).

Test results: As soon as the test is over, you will get your test results. You will receive a pass notice letter if you are successful, which you must submit with your citizenship application.

Retaking the test: You have seven days to repeat the test if you don't pass the first time. The test price must be paid once more for each attempt, though.

It's crucial to keep in mind that passing the Life in the UK test is just one of several prerequisites needed to become a citizen of the UK. Along with completing the English language requirements, you must also have no severe criminal convictions and be able to demonstrate that you have a solid understanding of UK culture.

The UK is full of surprises. It's the country that brought us tea, the Queen, and British accents. The United Kingdom is a deeply fascinating place for aspiring citizens to live in and for those just looking to explore.

But if you're not a British citizen, you can't just move here and automatically become a resident here. The test to get the UK citizenship works in a certain way. There are different procedures depending on whether you are 18 or over and whether you are under 18. So let's dive into the subject.

Immigrants who want to obtain British citizenship must consist of different requirements and procedures that vary according to the applicant's situation (under 18 or over 18 years old).

The Most Important Checklist for UK Citizenship

The law states that to be eligible for British citizenship, you need to be a child born in the UK. Also, you must have met all the requirements set by the law to qualify for British citizenship. To meet these requirements, there are two main things to keep in mind:

You MUST have a residency document from the UK (i.e. a UK National Insurance Number or a birth certificate).

You MUST have lived in the UK for at least five years.

If you have at least 3 out of the four requirements, you can start the naturalization process. If not, you cannot apply for a British Citizenship through Naturalization process. If your residency document is incomplete, or if you failed to meet some of the five-year requirement, you cannot even go to submit your application to be a British citizen.

The UK citizenship test is set to make sure that you meet the criteria set by the law. If you can't meet the test for citizenship, it means that you are unable to apply for a British Citizenship.

How To Apply to Become A British Citizen?

If you are a citizen living in the UK, you should know that there are different ways to apply for a passport and one of these ways is through Naturalization. You can find a complete tutorial on how to apply for a home county here.

First, you need to check if you meet the criteria. To do so, visit our website and take our free eligibility test . After that, you can start filling in your application. You will have to send all the necessary documents we ask for. Once this has been done, we will pass your application onto a government agency for review.

After several weeks or months (it can take up to 12 months), you will get a letter saying if you have passed the test or not. But just like the earlier mentioned process, this can take up to 12 months before you get to know if you have passed the test.

If You Have Passed The UK Citizenship Test

Once you have passed the test, be ready for the next step. You will then need to pass the interview for naturalization. This might not be easy because there are people who have a very hard time passing through it. But the good news is that you do not have to wait long. There are three different types of interviews:

The interview held by the UK citizenship examiner The interview with a panel of UK citizenship judges The Home Office persuasive public general naturalization examination

All these three interviews take from 3 to 4 hours and requires you to answer all questions thoroughly. The interview with a panel of judges can be done by video conference as well.

Once you have passed all the interviews, you will be issued with a certificate of citizenship. All you need to do to keep this is to renew your passport.

And that's how the test works to become a British citizen. It will take some time and effort on your part, but in the end it will all result in having a British passport, hence the phrase "passport to life. "

UK Citizenship Test – How To Apply For a British Passport Step 1: The Eligibility test for a British passport When you wish to become a British citizen, the first thing you need to do is take our free eligibility test . This tests your knowledge of the UK and its national life, as well as your knowledge of citizenship and naturalisation in the UK. Our 100% free eligibility test will ensure that you are ready to apply for your citizenship. Step 2: How to apply for a UK passport application Once you have passed the naturalization test, you can start to fill in your app...

How To Apply For A British Passport? If You Have Already Passed the Test The next step is applying for a British passport. You can do this just like all other applicants, by filling out an application form and sending it off to the embassy or consulate where you want to collect it. Our free e-Book on how to apply for a British passport has all the info you need. We will cover some of the most common questions here. You cannot get your UK passport online. This is a fast and reliable method, but it is not the only one. You have to apply in person at your local office. Use the contact details below to look up your local embassy/consulate. Doing this yourself gives you extra chances to be successful when applying for a British passport. How long does the application process for an application for a British passport take? This depends on several factors, such as how many pages your application contains, what the procedure costs and how you apply for a UK passport.

BONUS:
Practical Tests To Pass Exam

How to prepare for the test

1. Study the materials

The first and most important step of your preparations is to study the complete official study materials. These are found in the Home Office handbook, Life in the United Kingdom: A guide for new residents and are reproduced in our titles, Life in the UK Test: Study Guide 2021 and Life in the UK Test: Handbook 2021.

It is essential that you read and understand the testable chapters before taking your test. Taking practice tests alone will not prepare you for the real test.

2. Take practice tests

Once you've finished thoroughly reviewing the study materials, you should check if you are ready to take the test by completing the practice tests from this book.

When you sit your official test, you will be given 45 minutes to complete the test. So when you take a practice test, you should allow yourself the same time. The pass mark in the official test is at least 75% – or up to six incorrect answers. Again, this is what you should aim to score when you take a practice test.

If you can consistently score at least 75% and finish a test within 45 minutes, then you are ready to take your official test.

If you do not pass the practice tests satisfactorily and do not feel confident enough to sit your official test you should continue your study of the testable materials. If you do not have sufficient time left before your test to do more study, then you may be able to reschedule your test appointment. You can reschedule your test without charge up to seven days before the date. If you cancel your booking with less than seven days' notice, your booking fee will not be refunded.

3.   Online tests

Once you've finished testing yourself using the questions in this book, you can go online and access further tests with our free subscription offer.

WARNING: DO NOT MEMORISE QUESTIONS

The practice questions contained in this book are intended to help you assess your understanding of the study materials and check if you are ready to take the official test.

Do not prepare for the test by memorizing the questions in this book.

All the questions are in the same format as the official test questions. But they are not identical to the questions in the official test. The Home Office regularly revises the wording of questions used in the Life in the UK Test.

It is very important that you fully read and understand the study materials before taking your test.

TEST

Question 1

Which TWO British fighter aircraft took part in the Battle of Britain?

    A. Hurricane

    B. Vulcan

    C. Spitfire

    D. Dornier

Question 2

Is the statement below True or False?

In the English Civil War those who supported the king were called 'Cavaliers'

    A. True

    B. False

Question 3

Which TWO of the people below are famous British inventors?

    A. Bradley Wiggins

    B. John Logie Baird

    C. Gustav Holst

    D. Frank Whittle

Question 4

When is Boxing Day?

- A. 24 December
- B. 25 December
- C. 26 December
- D. 27 December

Question 5

Which of these statements is correct?

- A. Tudor King Henry VIII is famous for breaking away from the Church of Rome and marrying six times.
- B. Tudor King Henry VIII is famous for his successful victory against the French at the battle of Agincourt.

Question 6

Which of these statements is correct?

- A. You need to be at least 17 years of age to drive a car or motorcycle.
- B. You need to be at least.18 years of age to drive a car or motorcycle.

Question 7

Which body created the European Convention on Human Rights?

- A. The United Nations
- B. The European Union
- C. The Council of Europe

D. The North Atlantic Treaty Organisation

Question 8

Which of these statements is correct?

A. Today girls leave school, on average with better qualifications than boys
B. Today girls leave school, on average with poorer qualifications than boys.

Question 9

In the 2009 citizenship ceremony what proportion of people identified themselves as Christian?

A. Ten per cent (10%)
B. Thirty per cent (30%)
C. Fifty per cent (50%)
D. Seventy per cent (70%)

Question 10

Is the statement true below True or False?

Margaret Thatcher was Britain's first woman Prime Minister

A. True
B. False

Question 11

Which of these statements is correct?

A. In the 1840s there was a famine in Ireland and more than a million people died.

B. In the 1970s there was a famine in Ireland and more than a million people died.

Question 12

Which are the TWO homes of the Prime Minister?

A. 10 Downing Street

B. Chequers

C. 11 Downing Street

D. Marble Arch

Question 13

Name the TWO scientists that developed penicillin into a usable drug?

A. Clement Attlee

B. Howard Florey

C. Ernst Chain

D. Roald Dahl

Question 14

St David is the Patron Saint of which country?

A. Wales

B. England

C. Scotland

D. Northern Ireland

Question 15

Who chairs debates in the House of Commons?

    A. The Prime Minister

    B. The Speaker

    C. The Chancellor of the Exchequer

    D. The Leader of the Opposition

Question 16

The Wars of the Roses was fought between which TWO families?

    A. The House of York

    B. The House of Windsor

    C. The House of Lancaster

    D. The House of MacDonald

Question 17

When did women get the right to vote at 21, the same age as men?

    A. 1857

    B. 1918

    C. 1928

    D. 1960

Question 18

Which of these statements is correct?

    A. People under 18 are not allowed to participate in the National Lottery

    B. People under 16 are not allowed to participate in the National Lottery

Question 19

Which of these statements is correct?

A. William of Orange defeated James II at the Battle of Culloden in Scotland
B. William of Orange defeated James II at the Battle of the Boyne in Ireland

Question 20

Is the statement below True or False?

Members of the army are allowed to stand for public office.

A. True
B. False

Question 21

Is the statement below True or False?

Cricket is the UK's most popular sport..

A. True
B. False

Question 22

Is the statement below True or False?

Female genital mutilation is illegal in the UK

A. True
B. False

Question 23

Is the statement below True or False?

The Church of England is a Roman Catholic Church

    A. True

    B. False

Question 24

Is the statement below True or False

The British Constitution is written down in a single document.

    A. True

    B. False

Test Two

Q1. Who was Henry VII's son?

    a) Richard IV

    b) Henry VIII

    c) Edward III

    d) John II

Q2. In which city did Sake Dean Mahomet own up the first curry house in Britain in 1810?

    a) Birmingham

    b) London

    c) Dublin

d) Liverpool

Q3. On which two of these cities did the United States drop atomic bombs, bringing the Second World War to a close?

a) Berlin
b) Hamburg
c) Hiroshima
d) Nagasaki

Q4. In what area of England is Land's End situated?

a) South west
b) North east
c) North west
d) South east

Q5. Who was Churchill's deputy Prime Minister in the wartime coalition government?

a) Clement Attlee
b) Anthony Eden
c) Harold Macmillan
d) Neville Chamberlain

Q6. Who wrote Land of Hope and Glory?

a) Henry Purcell
b) George Handel
c) Gustav Holst
d) Edward Elgar

Q7. The UN was formed after which conflict?

   a) The Boer War

   b) The First World War

   c) The liberation of Kuwait

   d) The Second World War

Q8. Which two of these statements are true?

   a) The first people to live in Britain were hunter-gatherers

   b) The first people to live in Britain were farmers

   c) In the Stone Age, Britain was connected to the continent by a land bridge

   d) In the Bronze Age, Britain was connected to the continent by a land bridge

Q9. The 'Ulster Fry' meal is traditional in which country?

   a) England

   b) Wales

   c) Scotland

   d) Northern Ireland

Q10. What are the age limits on becoming a school Governor?

   a) You must be over 21

   b) You must be over 21 and under 60

   c) You must be over 18 and under 65

   d) You must be over 18

Q11. Which one of these statements about the Queen is false?

   a) She succeeded her mother

b) She opens the parliamentary session

c) All Acts of parliament are made in her name

d) She is married to Prince Philip, the Duke of Edinburgh

Q12. Universities in which two British cities were involved in work on the structure of the DNA molecule?

a) Oxford

b) York

c) London

d) Cambridge

Q13. What was William Wilberforce famous as?

a) An abolitionist

b) A slave trader

c) An inventor

d) An explorer

Q14. Sir Ian Botham captained which English team?

a) Football

b) Rugby

c) Cycling

d) Cricket

Q15. Charles II was succeeded by James II. What religion did James follow?

a) Puritanism

b) Presbyterianism

c) Protestantism

d) Roman Catholicism

Q16. Which one of these facts about shopping locally is false?

a) Shopping locally helps businesses and farmers in your area
b) Shopping locally helps businesses and farmers in Britain
c) Shopping locally is always cheaper
d) Shopping locally reduces your 'carbon footprint' as your goods have not travelled so far

Q17. Which one of these cities is not in England?

a) Liverpool
b) Sheffield
c) Newport
d) Norwich

Q18. The government is formed by:

a) The party most favoured by the monarch
b) The party with a majority of MPs
c) The party with the most members in the House of Lords
d) The party with the most MPs and members in the House of Lords

Q19. In what month are council elections normally held?

a) April
b) May
c) September
d) October

Q20. Who designed the new St Paul's Cathedral?

a) Inigo Jones

b) Sir Christopher Wren

c) Robert Adam

d) Sir Normal Foster

Q21. What time do pubs usually open on Mondays to Saturdays?

a) 10 am

b) 11 am

c) 2 pm

d) 3pm

Q22. Once a person has reached the age limit at which they can use their driving licence, how long is their new licence valid for?

a) 1 year at a time

b) 3 years at a time

c) 4 years at a time

d) 5 years at a time

Q23. What is the name of the best preserved prehistoric village in northern Europe?

a) Stonehenge

b) Skara Brae

c) Maiden Castle

d) Orkney

Q24. The paper on which you mark your vote is called

a) A ballot paper

b) A ballot card

c) A polling card

d) A voting paper

Test Three

a) Q1. Why was Mary Queen of Scots executed?

a) She was suspected of involvement in her husband's murder

b) She was suspected of plotting against Elizabeth I

c) She made Roman Catholic services illegal

d) She handed the throne to her Protestant son, Edward VI

Q2. The 1960s was a period of great social change. What name is sometimes given to the 1960s?

a) The Socialist Sixties

b) The Liberal Sixties

c) The Swinging Sixties

d) The Rebel Sixties

Q3. In what two months can Diwali fall?

a) April or May

b) May or June

c) September or October

d) October or November

Q4. For which two monarchs did Sir William Walton write coronation marches?

a) George V

b) Queen Victoria

c) George VI

d) Elizabeth II

Q5. In which year was the voting age reduced to 18 for men and women?

a) 1949

b) 1959

c) 1969

d) 1979

Q6. On what date is St. George's Day?

a) 1st March

b) 1st April

c) 21st March

d) 23rd April

Q7. In what year did Concorde begin to carry passengers?

a) 1965

b) 1969

c) 1976

d) 1978

Q8. Who did the Scottish Jacobites attempt to put on the throne in 1745?

a) James II's son

b) William III's son

c) James II's grandson

d) George I's grandson

Q9. Which of these citizens would not be allowed to stand for office as an MP?

a) A British citizen

b) An Irish citizen

c) A Commonwealth citizen

d) A citizen of another EU country

Q10. What is the national flower of Wales?

a) The poppy

b) The daffodil

c) The shamrock

d) The rose

Q11. Which two of these groups cannot stand for election?

a) Members of the armed forces

b) Members of the police

c) Health Service workers

d) Civil servants

Q12. Members of the House of Lords may not stand for election to the House of Commons.

a) True

b) False

Q13. Which UK act incorporated the European Convention of Human Rights?

a) The Human Rights Act

b) The Bill of Rights

c) The UK Rights Act

d) The European Human Rights Amendment

Q14. On which day do lovers or secret admirers send cards and gifts?

a) April Fool's Day

b) Boxing Day

c) Valentine's Day

d) Christingle

Q15. Which one of these expressions does not come from cricket?

a) 'Rain stopped play'

b) 'Batting on a sticky wicket'

c) 'Hole in one'

d) 'Playing a straight bat'

Q16. How many member countries does the UN have?

a) 50

b) 123

c) 175

d) 190

Q17. The Gaelic language is spoken in parts of which country?

a) Ireland

b) Wales

c) England

d) Scotland

Q18. The Bruce was written in the newly developed Scots language. What was it about?

a) Robert the Bruce's life

b) Geoffrey Chaucer's life

c) The Battle of Bannockburn

d) The Battle of Hastings

Q19. Who was in charge of the British fleet at the Battle of Trafalgar?

a) King George III

b) The Duke of Wellington

c) Admiral Nelson

d) William Wilberforce

Q20. What percentage of the UK population lives in England?

a) 44%

b) 52%

c) 66%

d) 84%

Q21. What is Sutton Hoo?

a) The site of a battle

b) A fort on Hadrian's Wall

c) The burial place of a king

d) A monastery on the island of Iona

Q22. Which of Shakespeare's plays contains the line 'To be or not to be?'

a) Hamlet

b) Romeo and Juliet

c) Macbeth

d) Henry V

Q23. Which one of these is not a fashion designer?

a) Clarice Cliff
b) Mary Quant
c) Vivienne Westwood
d) Alexander McQueen

Q24. Which film franchise was based on books by J.K Rowling and is one of the two highest-grossing film franchises?

a) Star Wars
b) Harry Potter
c) James Bond
d) Indiana Jones

Corrected Answers To Practical Tests

Test One

Question 1 = A, C

Question 2 = A

Question 3 = B, D

Question 4 = C

Question 5 = A

Question 6 = A

Question 7 = C

Question 8 = A

Question 9 = D

Question 10 = A

Question 11 = A

Question 12 = A, B

Question 13 = B, C

Question 14 = A

Question 15 = B

Question 16 = A,C

Question 17 = C

Question 18 = B

Question 19 = B

Question 20 = B

Question 21 = B

Question 22 = A

Question 23 = B

Question 24 = B

Test Two Answers

Q1. Who was Henry VII's son?

Answer: b)

Q2. In which city did Sake Dean Mahomet own up the first curry house in Britain in 1810?

Answer: b)

Q3. On which two of these cities did the United States drop atomic bombs, bringing the Second World War to a close?

Answer: c) & d)

Q4. In what area of England is Land's End situated?

Answer: a)

Q5. Who was Churchill's deputy Prime Minister in the wartime coalition government?

Answer: a)

Q6. Who wrote Land of Hope and Glory?

Answer: d)

Q7. The UN was formed after which conflict?

Answer: d)

Q8. Which two of these statements are true?

Answer: a) & c)

Q9. The 'Ulster Fry' meal is traditional in which country?

Answer: d)

Q10. What are the age limits on becoming a school Governor?

Answer: d)

Q11. Which one of these statements about the Queen is false?

Answer: a)

Q12. Universities in which two British cities were involved in work on the structure of the DNA molecule?

Answer: c) & d)

Q13. What was William Wilberforce famous as?

Answer: a)

Q14. Sir Ian Botham captained which English team?

Answer: d)

Q15. Charles II was succeeded by James II. What religion did James follow?

Answer: d)

Q16. Which one of these facts about shopping locally is false?

Answer: c)

Q17. Which one of these cities is not in England?

Answer: c)

Q18. The government is formed by:

Answer: b)

Q19. In what month are council elections normally held?

Answer: b)

Q20. Who designed the new St Paul's Cathedral?

Answer: b)

Q21. What time do pubs usually open on Mondays to Saturdays?

Answer: b)

Q22. Once a person has reached the age limit at which they can use their driving license, how long is their new license valid for?

Answer: b)

Q23. What is the name of the best preserved prehistoric village in northern Europe?

Answer: b)

Q24. The paper on which you mark your vote is called

Answer: a)

Test Three Answers

Q1. Why was Mary Queen of Scots executed?

Answer: b)

Q2. The 1960s was a period of great social change. What name is sometimes given to the 1960s?

Answer: c)

Q3. In what two months can Diwali fall?

Answer: d)

Q4. For which two monarchs did Sir William Walton write coronation marches?

Answer: c) & d)

Q5. In which year was the voting age reduced to 18 for men and women?

Answer: c)

Q6. On what date is St. George's Day?

Answer: d)

Q7. In what year did Concorde begin to carry passengers?

Answer: c)

Q8. Who did the Scottish Jacobites attempt to put on the throne in 1745?

Answer: a)

Q9. Which of these citizens would not be allowed to stand for office as an MP?

Answer: d)

Q10. What is the national flower of Wales?

Answer: b)

Q11. Which two of these groups cannot stand for election?

Answer: a) & d)

Q12. Members of the House of Lords may not stand for election to the House of Commons.

Answer: a)

Q13. Which UK act incorporated the European Convention of Human Rights?

Answer: a)

Q14. On which day do lovers or secret admirers send cards and gifts?

Answer: c)

Q15. Which one of these expressions does not come from cricket?

Answer: c)

Q16. How many member countries does the UN have?

Answer: d)

Q17. The Gaelic language is spoken in parts of which country?

Answer: d)

Q18. The Bruce was written in the newly developed Scots language. What was it about?

Answer: c)

Q19. Who was in charge of the British fleet at the Battle of Trafalgar?

Answer: c)

Q20. What percentage of the UK population lives in England?

Answer: d)

Q21. What is Sutton Hoo?

Answer: c)

Q22. Which of Shakespeare's plays contains the line 'To be or not to be?'

Answer: a)

Q23. Which one of these is not a fashion designer?

Answer: a)

Q24. Which film franchise was based on books by J.K Rowling and is one of the two highest-grossing film franchises?

Answer: b)

Conclusion

If you plan on staying in the UK and want to live as a permanent resident, or if you have been living in the UK for more than 5 years, this guide is your one-stop-shop. It contains information on everything from registering a charity to marrying someone who's not a British citizen.

Thanks for purchasing the book.

Printed in Great Britain
by Amazon

31149934R00057